The Cry of Jabez

How a centuries-old prayer could transform your life

My Anointed Quill

My Anointed Quill Publishing

To God be the glory, great things He hath done!

SCRIPTURE

1 Chronicles 4:9–10 (KJV)—And Jabez was more honourable than his brethren: and his mother called his name Jabez, saying, Because I bare him with sorrow.

And Jabez called on the God of Israel, saying, Oh that thou wouldest bless me indeed, and enlarge my coast, and that thine hand might be with me, and that thou wouldest keep me from evil, that it may not grieve me! And God granted him that which he requested.

More Is _Not_ Always Better

And Jabez was more honourable than his brethren: and his mother called his name Jabez, saying, Because I bare him with sorrow.

At first glance, we're left with the impression that Jabez was a very blessed and set-apart child. After all, the Bible calls him "honourable." But let's do our homework and take a look at the intended meaning behind this word. According to the Hebrew lexicon,[1] the word honourable has four different meanings/interpretations in the Word of God.

1. The original Hebrew word is _adar_ (pronounced "aw-dar") which means "to be great, be majestic, wide, noble (poetic)." As defined above, three instances[2] exist in the Bible.

2. The original Hebrew word is _howd_ (pronounced "hode"), which means "splendour, majesty, vigour." In this context, 24 instances[3] exist in the Bible.

3. The original Hebrew word is _kabowd_ (pronounced "kaw-bode"), which means "glory, honour, glorious, abundance." In this context, 189 instances[4] exist in the Bible.

4. The original Hebrew word is _kabad_ (pronounced "kaw-bad," long "a" as in "laid"), which means

5

"to be heavy, be weighty, be grievous, be hard, be rich, be honourable, be glorious, be burdensome, be honoured." In this context, 112 instances[5] exist in the Bible—of which 1 Chronicles 4:9 is one! So now we discover that when Jabez was called honourable in the Bible, it was not because he was majestic or glorious. It was because he was a weighty, grievous, and burdensome child (and we need not go to the dictionary to know that none of these words are positive adjectives).

Why is it that of all the meanings listed, "honourable" in this instance cannot be "rich, honourable, glorious, honoured" (as in God especially favored him)? The second part of the verse tells us why—in fact, it is why he was called Jabez: "because I bare him with sorrow," said the mother in the second half of verse 9. There has been speculation as to why exactly the pregnancy was so sorrowful. Understanding the meaning of the word "honourable" gives us a clear clue. Putting the verse in laymen's terms, here's what we have: "And Jabez was more weighty, grievous, and burdensome than his brothers, so his mother called him Jabez because she said, 'I bore him with a lot of pain'" (according to this same lexicon,[6] Jabez means "sorrow").

What a challenge to start life with a name that tells everyone who hears it just what your mother thought of you when she gave birth to you! To be taunted and teased and judged before you ever get to utter a word. That was Jabez's fate. But—praise God—the story doesn't end there! Without spoiling the lessons ahead, this one verse tells us this: we cannot control the circumstances in which we are born. We can't even pick and choose what family or what parents get to rear us (or not). Though our upbringing—even our very name and all the connotations behind it—may seemingly doom us to a pain-filled life, with God (the Author and Finisher of our faith), the story does not need to follow the predetermined path chosen by our parents or our circumstance.

What does that mean? Just because we may be born to parents who were alcoholics or addicts and their parents and their parents' parents were the same, does not mean we are doomed to repeat their mistakes. These "genetic predispositions" (or as the Bible terms them, *sins of the Father passed down to the third and fourth generation*[7]) are meant to be destroyed, broken, done away with. There is always hope! God is in the miracle-working business, and neither our past nor our family's past determines who I AM THAT I AM predestined us to be!

Making Ourselves Heard

And Jabez called on the God of Israel...

Now that we understand Jabez's background, we can examine the text in verse 10 piece by piece...

Would you be surprised to hear that what we've come to know as the Prayer of Jabez is not a prayer at all? Yes, it's a radical statement, but still valid. Where's the proof? Well, when we're trying to get someone's attention, what's the first thing we do? Call them by name. Now unless they're standing right in front of us, it's unlikely that we'll softly call their name or say it barely above a whisper. We project and raise our voice to get their attention! Surely, if the Bible meant to say, "Jabez *prayed to* the God of Israel," it would have said just that. If we take a look at the same Hebrew lexicon we examined in part 1, we find that the word "called" as specified in this verse is qara (pronounced "kaw-raw") in Hebrew. There are three definitions[8] in the lexicon, none of which reference prayer!

Look up "call" in Merriam-Webster online, and we find two definitions. The one which applies is the first: *to speak in a loud distinct voice so as to be heard at a distance.*[9]

So, if we picture Jabez in our mind's eye as described in the Bible, we see him not praying to the Father but crying out, even shouting out to him! It was a cry of urgency, one that can be likened to the cry of blind Bartimaeus[10] when he knew Jesus was in his neighborhood. He didn't ask someone to get his attention; he cried out, "Jesus, thou son of David, have mercy on me!" And the more they told him to shut up, the louder he called out to Jesus.

Does this mean we're to dismiss the Prayer of Jabez altogether because it's not technically a prayer? Not at all. But there is a greater overarching meaning than adopting it as a daily prayer. Often, prayer is viewed/illustrated as a quiet, pious act that we pray in our minds to God the Father. We kneel before God, and we close our eyes, and we pour out our hearts telepathically.

This one line in 1 Chronicles 4:10 is seeking to bring us a mighty revelation: there are certain things we require of God that necessitate that we cry out to Him. We have to put away our pious persona and get down to the most basic and guttural cry of our hearts. Jabez was keenly aware of this. He spent his entire childhood "enjoying" the ridicule and scorn of his name. At one point, he said, "enough is enough!" He didn't care who heard nor who was looking. He cried out loudly to the "God of Israel."

What's the importance behind the Bible's need to clearly identify whom he cried out to? In the backdrop of Jabez's time, idol worship was rampant. Multiple gods existed that many worshiped. By definition, in the Hebrew lexicon, "God of Israel" literally means "the one true God prevails." Matthew Henry's commentary said it best in the following quote: *Jabez [cried out] to the living and true God, who alone can hear and answer prayer; and, in prayer, he regarded Him as a God in covenant with His people.*[11] So there was no misunderstanding or ambiguity or doubt whom Jabez was crying to—especially to those who might have been within earshot. The Bible makes it very explicit.

Oh that we would daily have the courage to ***cry out*** unto the one true God who prevails so He may rain down upon us His richest blessings!

It's All About the Little Things

Oh that thou wouldest bless me indeed…

Taking this portion of the verse at face value, we know that Jabez wanted God to bless him. But what did that mean? We bless our food, we bless those who sneeze around us, and we say "God bless" to friends and loved ones. Ever stopped to consider what we're invoking by inserting the word "bless" or any of its variations in our prayers, our writing, our speech?

Three definitions in Merriam-Webster[12] stand out and really speak to the intent. The first, "to invoke divine care for [as in when someone sneezes]." The second, "to confer prosperity or happiness upon." The third, "endow, favor." In layman's terms, blessings are God's showers of divinely supernatural care, success, happiness, and favor that he rains down ("endows") upon us. When we call upon God to bless us or others, that is what we ask for, on our behalf or theirs.

So now we have a clearer picture of just what Jabez was asking of God when he cried out, "Lord of Israel, [faithful and true], bless me!" An interesting point to keep in mind shared by Bruce Wilkinson[13]: asking for a blessing in this particular way took an extraordinary amount of trust. Why, you ask? After all, who wouldn't want God's showers of divinely supernatural care, success, happiness, and favor to rain down upon them? The trust shines through in a critical but important omission: Jabez asked for God to bless him, but he left it entirely up to God to decide how.

Often, it's so easy to overlook God's blessings because they don't take on the form of what we may think a typical/traditional blessing ought to. For example, sometimes, we can miss the blessings that aren't financial. Maybe we eat Ramen Noodles for an entire week and grumble about the dietary "rut," but we overlook the blessing of having food while over 1 billion of the world's population go hungry. We exasperate over the cramped studio apartment while in the past year alone, 150 million of the world's citizens were completely homeless[14]—so we miss the blessing of a roof over our heads.

So today and every day, dear reader, let us resolve within our hearts and minds to emulate Jabez: ask Jehovah Jireh—He who knows that which we need before we even ask and longs to do for us beyond our wildest imaginations (Matthew 6:25–33)—for His showers of divinely supernatural care, success, happiness, and favor to rain down upon us ... let Him worry about the what, when, where, and the how of those supernatural showers!

The Glory in Begging

Oh that thou wouldest bless me indeed…

We could learn a thing or two from a beggar. Yes, no error—press rewind—*we could learn a thing or two from a beggar.* Granted, it's not something we aspire to as children. Certainly not something to aspire to in our later years, but what exactly can a beggar teach us? Their stock and trade, of course! It's safe to assume that not every person that walks past a beggar gives them money—else they'd not be beggars for long! But let's say that in an 8-hour "workday," a beggar comes in contact with 60 people. Of that 60, only one out of every five gives the beggar money. That's a whopping total of 12 people! Of that 12, the likelihood that even half will give that beggar $1 or more is quite slim.

Of course, we're not going to enter a long-drawn-out discussion of the virtues (or lack thereof) of begging. But here's what the beggar teaches. Whether he makes $12.50 all day or $0.50, drive or walk past that same route again tomorrow and guess what you'll find? The beggar! Put aside for a moment that he's not working for the money and whatever other reason why they'd be back there and think on this: the beggar might be rejected 48 of 60 times, but they'll continue begging (asking) for money on the chance that some will give (say yes). In short, they'll keep asking until somebody's giving!

Where's the relevance? After all, God is a merciful, loving Father who wants nothing more than to lavish on us, His children, to grant us the desires of our heart if we but delight in Him. So how in the world is the beggar analogy applicable? Well, have you asked of the LORD for every single thing you've ever wanted to ask of Him? *Every single thing*? Or can you think of some thing(s) that seemed just too far-fetched or silly to ask of Him? The Bible is full of scriptures that remind us that the key obstacle that stands in the way of us and the blessings the Father so richly wants to bestow is our failure to ask!

However, very unlike the street beggar, if we ask earnestly, with a sincere and pure heart—not for our own selfish, greedy motives or our own vainglory—the Lord answers yes 100% of the time. That is the secret to Jabez's success. He didn't ask of I AM THAT I AM thinking in himself: *Who am I to ask God these things? I don't deserve to ask that of Him! He's just going to say no anyway, so why bother?!* He cried out unto the Lord and asked for everything that his heart and soul desired. May we be brave enough to throw pride, caution, and prudence to the wind and come before the Lord and *ask* Him to rain down on us His richest blessings, for when we do, He'll fill our cup to overflowing!

Christians Without Borders

...enlarge my coast.

Now, this is where Jabez's cry really gets good! He's gone from making a general request to the God of Israel, to rain down His showers of divinely supernatural care, success, happiness, and favor on him, to a request we could all appreciate: "enlarge my coast." Or in the more common terms, "expand my territory." At some point or another, we've all made this request to the Father. Whether it was when seeking advancement/promotion at work, a bigger/better home, a bigger/nicer car, or even a larger ministry, these are all variations of the same request.

Does God honor/answer those requests? Absolutely. One of the most beautiful texts that affirms that is found in Matthew 7:9–11: *Which of you, if his son asks for bread, will give him a stone? Or if he asks for a fish, will give him a snake? If you, then, though you are evil, know how to give good gifts to your children, how much more will your Father in heaven give good gifts to those who ask him!* A heartwarming reminder that Jehovah Jireh, the Lord Our Provider, wants nothing more than to lavish good gifts on us, His children.

But let's think outside the box for a moment. What if, *what if* we decided to be more radical in our request? Surely, to ask of God what we want, we could be no bolder! But, what if instead of taking a page out of Jabez's book and making this exact request, we added a King Solomon twist?! In 1 Kings 3:5, the LORD came to Solomon in a dream. Clearly, Solomon was highly favored because the Lord asked him plain and simple, "Ask what I shall give thee." In other words, "Solomon, whatever you ask for, I'll give to you."

Solomon's desire was simple, and there was no hesitation on his part: wisdom to judge the Lord's people. That was all Solomon desired. The Lord granted that which he asked, but it doesn't end there. Verses 12 and 13 tell us the Lord's response to Solomon's request: *lo, I have given thee a wise and an understanding heart; so that there was none like thee before thee, neither after thee shall any arise like unto thee. **And I have also given thee that which thou hast not asked, both riches, and honour: so that there shall not be any among the kings like unto thee all thy days.***

Solomon knew the real secret to the Lord's richest blessings: a heart longing for the things of the Lord. All Solomon wanted was the wisdom to execute the work which the Lord appointed him to. Because that was his one earnest desire, he activated the secret password, if you will, that unlocked the door to an unimaginable fountain of blessings over his life.

Our challenge today and every day is not to pray for the Lord to "enlarge our coast." Surely the LORD will honor that prayer, but let us consider and pray the following: *Lord, work through us so that your territory—as in your Kingdom—is enlarged. Give us the heart of Solomon: humble, sincere, and on fire for the things of you, that we forever seek only to expand in service for you. Lord, give us Solomon's heart so that all we ever truly want is for you to **enlarge your coast through us.** In Jesus' name we pray, amen.*

His Masterpieces

...that thine hand might be with me.

What do Michelangelo, da Vinci, Beethoven, and Einstein have in common? Their names are easily recognized for the legacy they left behind: through music, art, and science. Their work during their era had—and continues to have—such a profound effect on humanity that most of us can easily identify at least one of their masterpieces. They are not alone. There are countless gifted individuals whose handiwork has stood the test of time. Their creations—from Michelangelo's David, da Vinci's Mona Lisa, Beethoven's symphonies, and Einstein's Theory of Relativity—are a testament to their creativity, genius, and influence within their fields.

Yet long before they came along, the Master Craftsman's handiwork was on full display. All of creation—from the firmament above to the seas below—are a living witness to the wondrous works of His hands. We, who are His most marvelous handiwork, are the living, breathing testimonies of the most skillful—and only—creation made by His hands.

In the context of the Jabez story, his request becomes clearer. By asking for the Lord's hand, Jabez was saying: *Father, I want you ever so present in my life that anyone whom I come into contact with will know beyond the shadow of a doubt that you are the one behind all of my successes, riches, and blessings. I want to be a great masterpiece on display for your glory to win others to your kingdom.*

May we sincerely go before the throne of grace and ask the Father for His hand—not merely for the blessings—but more importantly, that He may come into our lives and, with His hands, mold and shape us into what He created us to be.

Our Evil Twins

…and that thou wouldest keep me from evil, that it may not grieve me!

Most of us have heard it said at one point or another: "it wasn't me! It was my evil twin!" Maybe we've even used it ourselves to justify/explain our less-than Godly behavior. Yes, it's good for laughs, but there's actually more truth behind this phrase than humor. It's a fact: we each all have a darker half we carry around. But what the world calls "evil twin," we as believers know more affectionately as "our flesh."

And whether we wish to admit it or not, we are **not** stronger than our flesh! When we presume ourselves to be, we find ourselves in a situation like Eve did in the garden, or David as he looked out of his balcony and lusted after Bathsheba (which led him to put out a hit on her husband so he could have her to himself). We could go on. How humbling to see that Jabez already knew himself well enough not to ask the Lord for the strength to resist evil but to avoid it altogether! It is then not surprising that when the disciples asked Jesus to teach them how to pray, one of the key phrases he recited was, "lead us *not into* [don't take us through] temptation, but deliver us *from* [keep it far away] evil." Even then, Jesus himself provided his disciples—men who walked with him every day, dined with him, saw him perform miracles firsthand until he left the earth—the key to overcoming evil: by choosing avoidance, the path of least resistance.

So, is it hopeless then? If our spirit man isn't stronger than our flesh, why bother? The answer is oh so simple: Jesus! We can do all things through him who gives us strength! Acknowledging we are weak on our own and if left to our own devices, we'd give in to the temptation is an expression of love to the Father. Our words might say, *God, I am not strong enough to resist x temptation, which leads me into y behavior, so keep it out of my way.* When translated through the Holy Spirit, the prayer heard by the Lord is, *Abba, I am sinful, and I am only strong enough when you abide in me. If you don't fight my battles for me, I won't win a single one. Please, Heavenly Daddy, stand in the gap and stop all temptations the enemy sends my way dead in their tracks!*

May we take a cue from Jabez and realize that having the power and strength to resist temptation is commendable, but having the wisdom to know it is better to avoid temptation, so we do not sin is even more honorable!

Knowledge + Faith = Limitless Power

...And God granted him that which he requested.

What was so great about Jabez that the writer of 1 Chronicles had to pause from recording the lineage of the "clan of Judah" to devote two verses of an otherwise strictly factual chapter to him? We can assume he was a descendant of Judah because he appears in this chapter, but his earthly father's identity is sketchy at best—yet there he appears, in all his splendor!

What made him so special? It wasn't his lineage nor what he did for a living, but it was what *he knew*. Jabez unlocked the secret to a life of bountiful blessings and the freedom from temptation *and* evil: speaking God's Word, to God! Somewhere along the way, someone or something reminded him of GOD's promise in Isaiah 55:11, "my word that goes out from my mouth: It will not return to me empty, but will accomplish what I desire and achieve the purpose for which I sent it."

Maybe he'd heard this promise all his life, but one day, he'd finally had enough of the rut he was in. He was finally fed up with his stuckness. Suddenly, he understood the magnitude of that promise. Then all the other promises in God's Word fell into place. He got the importance of calling upon things that be not as they may and praying back to the Father the statutes and promises in His Word.

But Jabez did more than understand the promise. He *believed* it with every fiber in his being. Jabez knew that it wasn't enough to know how to wield (handle, maneuver) the greatest weapon given to man—The Word—but it was equally important to have faith in The Word's ability to accomplish what it says it will, without a drop of doubt.

That is the first and only time we meet Jabez: at the cusp of walking into his destiny! There he stood, boldly before the throne of grace, without wavering, asking God all he desired for his life. He didn't hold back, and he didn't beat around the bush. And for that, God honored every one of his supplications. All of this because he presented The Word to God with faith, determination, and expectancy.

God wants to do unimaginably wonderful things in each and every one of our lives, just as in Jabez's, but we've got to act by requesting those things in faith and by uttering God's promises back to Him. Not because He needs reminding, but because they that ask, *believing*, receive.

My Anointed Quill

Works Cited

1. The KJV Old Testament Hebrew Lexicon. (n.d.). Accessed December 31, 2020. https://www.biblestudytools.com/lexicons/hebrew/kjv/.

2. "Adar." The KJV Old Testament Hebrew Lexicon. (n.d.). Accessed December 31, 2020. https://www.biblestudytools.com/lexicons/hebrew/kjv/adar.html.

3. "Howd." The KJV Old Testament Hebrew Lexicon. (n.d.). Accessed December 31, 2020. https://www.biblestudytools.com/lexicons/hebrew/kjv/howd.html.

4. "Kabowd." The KJV Old Testament Hebrew Lexicon. (n.d.). Accessed December 31, 2020. https://www.biblestudytools.com/lexicons/hebrew/kjv/kabowd.html.

5. "Kabad." The KJV Old Testament Hebrew Lexicon. (n.d.). Accessed December 31, 2020. https://www.biblestudytools.com/lexicons/hebrew/nas/kabad.html.

6. "Jabez." Bible Study Tools. (n.d.). Accessed December 31, 2020. https://www.biblestudytools.com/dictionaries/hitchcocks-bible-names/jabez.html.

7. Exodus 20:3-5, King James Version. Bible Gateway. (n.d.). Accessed December 31, 2020. https://www.biblegateway.com/passage/?search=Exodus%2020:3-5&version=KJV.

8. "Qara." The KJV Old Testament Hebrew Lexicon. Accessed December 31, 2020. https://www.biblestudytools.com/lexicons/hebrew/nas/qara.html.

9. "Call." Merriam-Webster.com. (n.d.). Accessed December 31, 2020. https://www.merriam-webster.com/dictionary/call.

10. Mark 10:46-52, King James Version. Bible Gateway. (n.d.). Accessed December 31, 2020. https://www.biblegateway.com/passage/?search=Mark+10%3A46-52&version=KJV.

11. 1 Chronicles 4. Matthew Henry's Commentary. (n.d.). Accessed December 31, 2020. https://biblehub.com/commentaries/mhc/1_chronicles/4.htm.

12. "Bless." Merriam-Webster.com. (n.d.). Accessed December 31, 2020. https://www.merriam-webster.com/dictionary/bless.

13. Wilkinson, Bruce H. (2000). *The Prayer of Jabez: Breaking Through to the Blessed Life.* Accessed December 31, 2020. https://www.amazon.com/Prayer-Jabez-Breakthrough-Wilkinson-Hardcover/dp/B00IGYVK56/ref=sr_1_4?dchild=1&keywords=prayer+of+jabez&qid=1609555609&sr=8-4.

14. Kuo, Gioietta. (2019 August). Yet another emerging global crisis—Homelessness. The Millennium Alliance for Humanity and the Biosphere. Accessed December 31, 2020. https://mahb.stanford.edu/library-item/yet-another-emerging-global-crisis-homelessness/#:~:text=Based%20on%20national%20reports%2C%20it's,population%2C%20may%20lack%20adequate%20housing.

Acknowledgment

I would be remiss if I did not take the time to recognize my better half, the one who has been by my side through sickness now health, through poorer now richer, through worse and now better.

Babe, without you, traveling this world would be a dark, lonely place. Thank you for believing in me when I didn't believe in myself and helping me realize my writing dreams.

May God continue to bless us 'til death do us part, or He comes to take us home.

Books in This Series

The MAQ Nuggets™ Collection. This series features books centered around biblical stories and concepts. Each book takes a closer look at topics or well-known stories in the Word of God, often from an overlooked lens.

The Cry of Jabez: How a centuries-old prayer could transform your life

The Cry of Jabez takes a deeper look at the prayer of Jabez and provides keen insights into its meaning and significance. Unlock the power of a prayer of old and step into the blessings God has in store for you.

Our Father: What an ancient, commonly recited prayer can still teach us today

The Lord's Prayer: known across the globe and recited by many. So what? *Our Father* deconstructs this well-known passage and reveals the relevance and power this prayer still holds today.

God's Full Armor: Where your real superpowers come from

Principalities. Powers. Rulers of the darkness of this world. Spiritual wickedness in high places. All terrifying, but what does it all mean? *God's Full Armor* demystifies these supernatural beings and provides a step-by-step guide to unlocking your most valuable weapons against them.

www.ingramcontent.com/pod-product-compliance
Lightning Source LLC
Chambersburg PA
CBHW021123020426
42331CB00004B/607